Milekah Speech Therapist
By Anne Swartz

This book is dedicated to
Jay Lose and Charles Lose
and Milekah Hebron.

Copyright @2023

All rights reserved. No part of this book may be reproduced or used in any manner without written permission of the copyright owner except for the use of quotations in a book review.

ISBN 979-8-9876520-0-8 (Paperback)
ISBN 979-8-9876520-1-5 (eBook)
Published by Aram Samsam Printing

Other titles by Anne Swartz
Nobody Likes Eddie, illustrated by Fred Dasinger
Who Wears A Beard?

Speech therapy is for anyone with an impediment, impairment, or any challenging speech or communication issue. Speech therapists also work on related topics, like swallowing and feeding disorders.

Everyone has ideas, but only some communicate in the same way. The speech therapist helps kids to find new ways to communicate.

All around the world kids communicate using languages. Languages are words and sounds in different combinations.

We might communicate with individual sounds, parts of words, whole words, sentences, paragraphs, or all together. We use words to write and tell stories.

Speech is different from language. Speech involves sound. Some kids easily speak, while others need help making sounds clearly or consistently.

Reading words aloud is a form of expressive language. When you read out loud, you speak and convey information to others via words and body language.

Receptive language is the understanding of words. It includes listening to what people say and occurs when you listen to sounds in a video game or a virtual reality environment.

Speech therapy happens in treatment sessions. The sessions might be one-on-one with a therapist, or the speech therapist meets in a group, in a classroom, in an office, or around a table.

Here's a speech therapist working with a child in a session, just the two. Speech therapy may look like playtime because the treatment may involve play. Sometimes speech therapy means that the child learns to label and identify things they already know and see all the time.

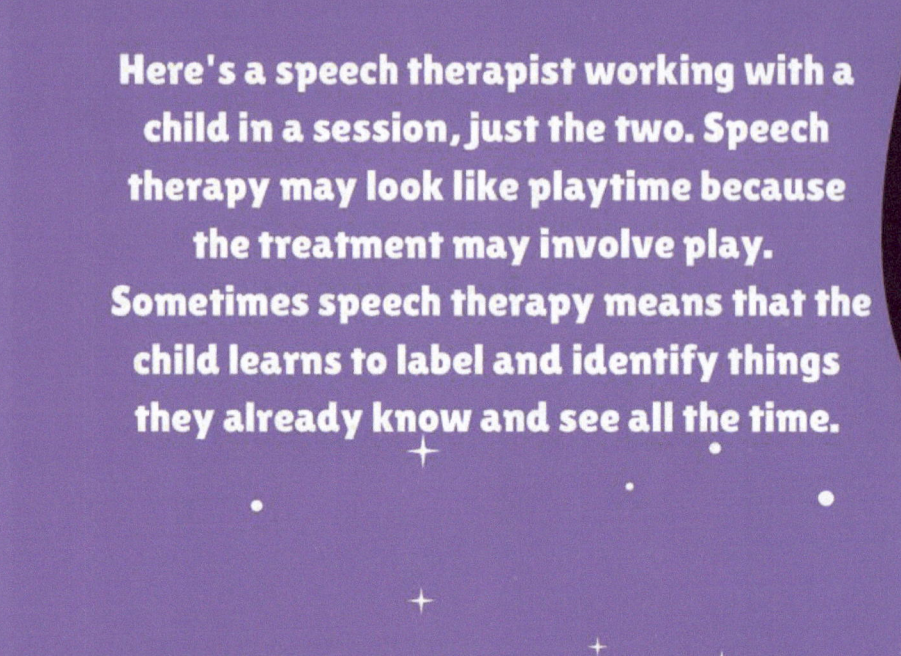

Speech therapists may also meet with your family to discuss speech and communication goals. Here is a therapist talking to a family. Families can add language into their routine to help children develop their speech skills, such as identifying or naming objects.

Your speech therapist might even meet with you virtually using the computer. The speech therapist can interact with you in real-time online. You might use headphones or speak directly to the therapist using the speaker and microphone on the computer.

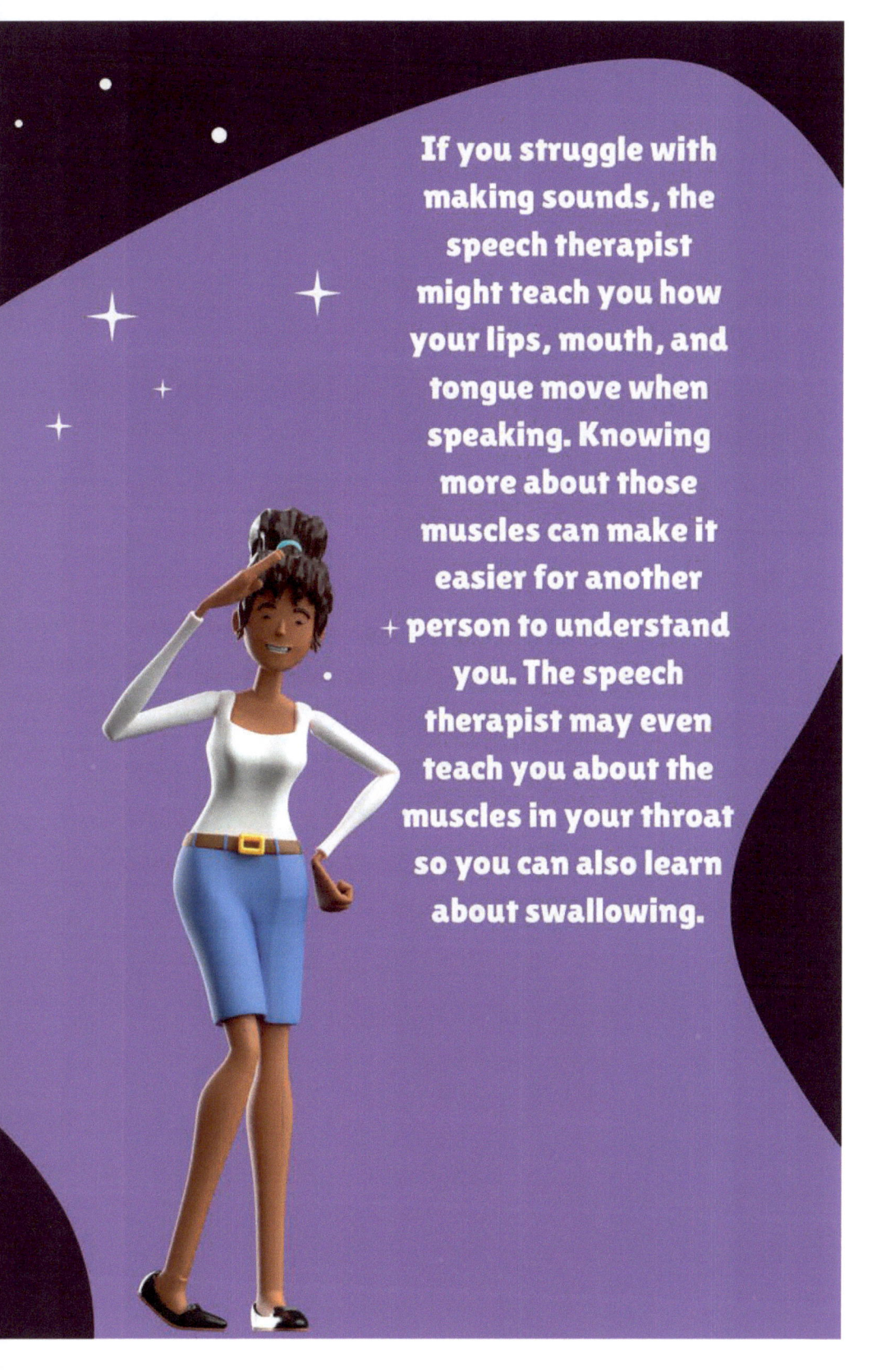

If you struggle with making sounds, the speech therapist might teach you how your lips, mouth, and tongue move when speaking. Knowing more about those muscles can make it easier for another person to understand you. The speech therapist may even teach you about the muscles in your throat so you can also learn about swallowing.

These two kids practice muscle exercises on their mouth and throat to help them swallow or speak more easily. Can you press your lips and talk? Do you feel how your mouth moves when you say words?

Your speech therapist may ask you to practice Oral Motor Exercises or OM exercises. These exercises will help strengthen your lips, mouth, and tongue muscles. They may seem funny, like making fish lips, or something unexpected, like drinking a thick milkshake from a straw.

The therapist might also guide you through making sounds. She might ask you to copy them while looking in the mirror. Having you watch yourself to see how you shape your mouth, lips, and tongue to form sounds will help you improve.

Milekah is excited and happy. She is expressing emotion. Some kids have difficulty expressing emotions. Children who need help learning about feelings might watch a video with a speech therapist to see how characters interact and show their feelings.

Speech therapists teach kids, and sometimes even their parents, functional communication, such as sign language, for specific goals like meeting needs or wants. Here is a boy who is learning the American Sign Language alphabet. He is making the sign for the letter B.

AAC devices are Augmentative Assistive Communication devices that help individuals with speech and language impairments communicate more effectively with technology. Even a computer can become an AAC device.

AAC devices include text communication, picture communication, or voice-generated communication. Milekah shows us small AAC devices here.

Phonics is one way you can learn to read and write. Phonics work by connecting sounds with letters.

This speech therapist and child are talking about how the letter k has several different possible sounds, such as <u>c</u>, <u>k</u>, <u>ch</u>, or <u>ck</u>. Learning about the connections between sounds and letters makes reading and writing much easier to understand.

Speech therapists work on helping kids to succeed in real-life situations with their families. Families then help kids bring skills home, such as kids who might need support with feeding because of difficulty swallowing.

Children also work on real-life skills with speech therapists by incorporating a picture schedule into the day. Organizing the day's activities can give a child an easy way to see what will happen and what has happened. It becomes something to talk about together.

www.ingramcontent.com/pod-product-compliance
Lightning Source LLC
Chambersburg PA
CBHW041744040426
42444CB00001B/25